POODLES

by Tammy Gagne

Consultant: Holly Corbett
Secretary, Twin Cities Poodle Club Inc.
Minneapolis, Minnesota

Capstone

Mankato, Minnesota

Edge Books are published by Capstone Press,
151 Good Counsel Drive, P.O. Box 669, Mankato, Minnesota 56002.
www.capstonepress.com

Books published by Capstone Press are manufactured with paper
containing at least 10 percent post-consumer waste.

Library of Congress Cataloging-in-Publication Data
Gagne, Tammy.
    Poodles / by Tammy Gagne.
    p. cm. — (Edge books. All about dogs)
    Includes bibliographical references and index.
    Summary: "Describes the history, physical features, temperament, and care
of the poodle breed" — Provided by publisher.
    ISBN 978-1-4296-3363-5 (library binding)
    1. Poodles — Juvenile literature. I. Title.
SF429.P85G34 2010
636.72'8—dc22   2008055922

Editorial Credits
Angie Kaelberer and Molly Kolpin, editors; Veronica Bianchini, designer;
    Marcie Spence, media researcher

Photo Credits
Alamy/DC/Photolink Ltd, 7; INTERFOTO Pressebildagentur, 9; Petra
    Wegner, 17
Capstone Press/Karon Dubke, cover, 1, 5 (both), 16, 20, 23, 27, 29
Cheryl A. Ertelt, 19
iStockphoto/Janalynn, 25 (bottom); majorosl, 12 (right); MoniqueRodriguez,
    25 (top); seattlematt, 28; stevedangers, 24; suemack, 13
Peter Arnold/Ullstein Bild, 11
Shutterstock/Andreas Gradin, 12 (left), 18; Glenda M. Powers, 21;
    Natalie V. Guseva, 15

Table of Contents

ONE SIZE DOES NOT FIT ALL

The poodle is one of the most easily recognized dog breeds. With its curly hair, this dog stands out among the crowd.

The poodle is the only dog breed to come in three different sizes. Standard poodles are the largest members of the breed. These poodles can be more than 26 inches (66 centimeters) tall at the **withers**. Toy poodles are the smallest members of the breed. Miniature poodles are larger than toys but smaller than standard poodles.

Both standard and miniature poodles are part of the American Kennel Club's (AKC) non-sporting group. Members of this group are usually kept as pets rather than as working dogs. Toy poodles belong to the toy group. This group includes the smallest breeds recognized by the AKC.

withers — the top of an animal's shoulders

The standard poodle (top) is larger than the miniature (left).

5

Is the Poodle for You?

Because the poodle comes in so many sizes, there is a poodle to suit almost any owner's needs. If you live in a small home or apartment, a toy poodle could be a perfect pet. If you like to stay physically fit, a standard poodle can make a great jogging partner. If you want a dog that isn't too big or too little, a miniature poodle might be for you.

Poodles get along well with children, but owners must teach kids how to treat dogs properly. Toy poodles need extra-gentle handling because of their tiny size. But even standard poodles must be treated with respect.

The best place to buy a poodle puppy is from a breeder. Responsible breeders work hard to produce healthy dogs with friendly **temperaments**. Adoption is another good choice. You can adopt a poodle through your local animal shelter or a poodle rescue group. Rescue groups help place unwanted dogs in new homes.

temperament — the combination of an animal's behavior and personality

Toy poodles don't require a big living space.

EDGE FACT

The English word "poodle" comes from the German word *pudel*. In German, this means "to splash in the water."

CHAPTER 2

POODLE HISTORY

Many people refer to the poodle as the French poodle. This is because poodles have been used for centuries as duck-hunting dogs in France. But the official name of the breed does not contain the word "French."

Most people think the breed began in Germany. The standard poodle is the oldest of the three poodle sizes. Dogs that look like standard poodles appear in German art and books from the 1400s.

Toy and miniature poodles have been around since the 1700s. They can be found in drawings by German artists from this time. European kings and queens often kept these dogs as pets, rather than as hunting dogs.

Hunting Dogs

All three types of poodles had abilities that made them good hunting dogs. Hunters valued standard and miniature poodles for their ability to move quickly through the water.

Toy poodles, on the other hand, did valuable work hunting truffles on land. A truffle is a fungus that grows in the ground. Truffles are considered tasty treats in many European countries. Poodles were trained to sniff for truffles. Smaller dogs did this job best because they didn't damage the truffle when digging for it.

Poodles as Performers

In the 1800s, traveling actors in Europe found another use for poodles. It was easy to train these intelligent dogs to do tricks for street shows and circuses. Poodles rode tricycles, balanced on tightropes, and walked on their front legs to entertain audiences.

Poodle Popularity

Poodles first arrived in the United States near the end of the 1800s. The AKC registered the first poodle owned by an American in 1886. At first, the breed did not receive much attention in the United States. But after the Poodle Club of America formed in 1931, the poodle became increasingly popular. By the 1950s, it was one of the most registered breeds in the country.

The poodle even made its mark on fashion. In the 1950s, many teenage girls owned poodle skirts. Each of these full, swaying skirts had a fabric poodle sewn on the front.

From 1960 to 1982, the poodle was the most popular breed in the United States. This is the longest period of time any breed has held this title. Today, the poodle remains one of the AKC's top 10 registered breeds.

Poodles were trained to perform in shows in the 1800s.

EDGE FACT

A dog that looks much like a poodle is pictured on a Roman coin from 111 BC.

Owners appreciate the poodle for its looks and its intelligence. Poodle owners can participate in many activities with their well-rounded pets. Dogs that closely match the AKC **breed standard** compete in dog shows. Poodles also show off their sharp wits in obedience trials. Other poodles enjoy participating in agility, tracking, hunting, and canine freestyle. Dogs run and jump over ramps and other equipment in agility contests. During tracking events, dogs must follow a person's scent. In canine freestyle, dogs compete in dancing contests along with their owners.

breed standard — the physical features of a breed that judges look for in a dog show

Poodles leap over obstacles in agility events.

13

CHAPTER 3

FLUFFY POMPONS AND BiG BRAINS

Size is the main feature that sets the standard, toy, and miniature poodle apart from one another. Standard poodles must be more than 15 inches (38 centimeters) tall at the withers. Most are 22 to 27 inches (56 to 69 centimeters) tall. Miniature poodles measure between 10 and 15 inches (25 and 38 centimeters). Poodles 10 inches (25 centimeters) or shorter are toy poodles. Whatever its size, a poodle should be well proportioned. The dog should be about as long as it is tall.

The Poodle Coat

Poodles competing in dog shows often look very different from pet poodles. Large sections of hair on a show poodle's body are shaved, while other areas are kept long. Fluffy pompons of fur are left on the ankles, hips, and tail. This hairstyle once had a practical purpose. Shaved areas made it easier for the poodle to move through water. Also, the pompons cover important organs like the kidneys. Because an animal's blood is filtered through its kidneys, the fur helps keep the dog warm.

The classic poodle cut was designed for speed and warmth.

Colors

Poodles come in several colors. The most common colors are black, white, and brown. Other colors include gray, blue, silver, red, and cream. Blue poodles are a blue-gray color. Red poodles are red-brown like the color of copper coins. Some colors sound a bit fancier than others. A peach-colored coat is called apricot. A café-au-lait poodle is light brown, similar to the color of coffee with cream. All poodles competing in dog shows must be a solid color, but some pet poodles are parti-color. These dogs have two or more colors in their coats.

Poodles do not shed as much as other dogs. Also, their coats are hypoallergenic. This means that people who are allergic to other dog breeds usually aren't bothered by a poodle's coat.

EDGE FACT

A poodle's color may change between birth and adulthood. Most silver dogs, for example, are black when they are born.

Faces and Tails

Poodles have dark, oval-shaped eyes. They are set far apart from each other. Some people think this gives the poodle an intelligent look.

A poodle's ears are long and hang close to the head. The hair on each ear is called fringe. On show dogs, the fringe shouldn't be much longer than the ear itself. Owners of pet poodles can clip this hair short or leave it as long as they like.

Poodle colors include (left to right) silver, apricot, black, and light apricot.

Most poodle breeders dock, or shorten, their puppies' tails soon after they are born. Like the haircut of show poodles, the original purpose for docking was to help with hunting. Shorter tails didn't get caught in brush and also helped the dogs steer through water. Show dogs in the United States must have docked tails. In some other countries, though, tail docking is illegal because people believe it is cruel.

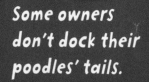

Some owners don't dock their poodles' tails.

Temperament

Many poodle fans think the poodle is the smartest of all dog breeds. Poodles of all sizes and ages are easy to train. They are also eager to learn and good at reading their owners' body language. Poodles know immediately when their owners are pleased or unhappy.

Some people make the mistake of thinking that smart dogs need less training. Smart dogs need just as much training as other pets. Poodles rely on their owners to teach them good behavior. Keep teaching your poodle new things even after it has learned all the basic commands. A bored poodle is more likely to misbehave.

Poodles are smart and easy to train.

Poodles are loyal dogs. They bond closely with their owners. For this reason, some people call the poodle a one-person dog. You can prevent your dog from getting too attached to you by socializing it. Introduce your poodle puppy to as many people and animals as possible. This will help create a friendly, secure dog.

EDGE FACT

Standard poodles live about 15 years. Toy and miniature poodles can live even longer.

CHAPTER 4

CARING FOR A POODLE

Poodles have a reputation for needing lots of pampering. But this breed is much easier to care for than many people think. Poodles aren't nearly as delicate as they seem. Even toy poodles like active play. All poodles do need to be groomed regularly. But pet poodles do not need constant brushing, clipping, and bathing like show dogs do.

Feeding

Feed your poodle a diet made for a dog its size. Standard poodles should eat food made for larger breeds. Feed your miniature or toy poodle food made for smaller dogs. Also, consider your dog's activity level. High-energy foods are perfect for active poodles like those that compete in agility contests. Diet formulas are best for overweight dogs.

Hard dog food helps clean the teeth. If you feed your poodle soft canned food, be prepared to brush its teeth more often. Plaque and tartar form more quickly on a dog's teeth when it eats canned food.

Owners should choose
food based on their dog's
size and activity level.

Exercise

All poodles need daily exercise. How much activity your dog needs depends on its size. Both standard and miniature poodles can go for long walks or even jogs. Toy poodles also need regular exercise, but their shorter legs don't allow them to run alongside their owners. A toy poodle can get enough exercise by running around indoors. But remember that fresh air is also healthy for your poodle. For dogs, a big part of a walk is getting to stop and smell the roses – and everything else along the way.

All types of poodles need daily exercise, like playing fetch.

Use shampoo made just for dogs on your poodle.

Grooming

Unless you plan to show your poodle, you may want to keep its fur in a pet clip. This shorter hairstyle will help prevent mats from forming. If you prefer the traditional haircut, be prepared to brush your dog every day. Otherwise, your dog must be brushed at least once a week.

How often to bathe your poodle also depends on whether your dog spends time in the show ring. A monthly bath should be enough to keep most poodles clean. But show dogs need to be bathed every week to keep up their appearance.

EDGE FACT

Always brush your poodle before bathing it. Any mats in a poodle's coat will become more tangled once they get wet.

Ears, Nails, and Teeth

Dogs with long ears, such as poodles, tend to get more ear infections than other breeds. To prevent this problem, clean your poodle's ears at least once each week. Use an ear wash solution and a cotton ball.

Clip your dog's nails every two to three weeks. Overgrown nails can get caught on clothing or carpeting. Finally, don't forget to brush your poodle's teeth. Even dogs that eat hard food should have their teeth cleaned every day. Whether you are brushing your dog's teeth or washing its fur, always use products made for dogs. Human products can make dogs sick.

Vet Visits

Poodles need to visit a veterinarian at least once a year. During the exam, the vet will weigh your dog, listen to its heartbeat, and check its joints. The vet will also give your dog any necessary **vaccinations**.

vaccination — a shot of medicine that protects animals from a disease

diabetes — a disease in which there is too much sugar in the blood

All types of poodles can have health problems. Toy and miniature poodles can suffer from food allergies and **diabetes**. Toy poodles also can suffer from hypoglycemia if they go too long without eating. Hypoglycemia is the medical term for low blood sugar. To prevent this problem, feed your toy dog several small meals each day instead of one large one.

Regular vet visits will help keep poodles healthy.

EDGE FACT

Toy poodles' teeth are often crowded in their small mouths, leaving places for plaque to build up. Regular dental care is even more important for these dogs.

Smart, playful poodles can be their owners' best friends.

Standard poodles also can have health problems. These larger poodles often suffer from kidney diseases and bloat. Bloat is a condition in which the stomach fills with gas that can't escape. If the stomach flips, it is known as bloat with torsion. Bloat can cause death. But vets can correct the problem with surgery if it's caught early. To help prevent bloat, don't allow your poodle to gulp down its food. Also, wait about two hours after a meal before exercising your dog.

To help your poodle live a long life, have it spayed or neutered. These operations prevent dogs from having puppies, which helps control the pet population. Spaying and neutering also reduces a dog's risk for illnesses like cancer.

With good care and training, a poodle makes a wonderful pet. This loyal breed adores its human family members. Few dogs will work harder to please you or will love you more.

Glossary

agility (uh-GI-luh-tee) — the ability to move fast and easily

body language (BAH-dee LANG-gwij) — the movements people use that show what they are thinking or feeling

breed standard (BREED STAN-durd) — the physical features of a breed that judges look for in a dog show

diabetes (dye-uh-BEE-teez) — a disease in which there is too much sugar in the blood

hypoallergenic (hye-poh-a-luhr-JEN-ik) — possessing a quality that reduces or eliminates allergic reactions

hypoglycemia (hye-poh-glye-SEE-mee-uh) — the medical term for low blood sugar

temperament (TEM-pur-uh-muhnt) — the combination of an animal's behavior and personality; the way an animal usually acts or responds to situations shows its temperament.

vaccination (vak-suh-NAY-shun) — a shot of medicine that protects animals from a disease

withers (WITH-urs) — the top of an animal's shoulders; a dog's height is measured from the ground to the withers.

Read More

Landau, Elaine. *Poodles Are the Best!* The Best Dogs Ever.
Minneapolis: Lerner, 2010.

MacAulay, Kelley, and Bobbie Kalman. *Poodles.*
Pet Care. New York: Crabtree, 2007.

Internet Sites

FactHound offers a safe, fun way to find Internet sites
related to this book. All of the sites on FactHound have been
researched by our staff.

Here's all you do:

Visit *www.facthound.com*

FactHound will fetch the best sites for you!

Index